I0157496

A Miracle Before Time

Story by Nati Carrillo

Illustrated by Sheila Alejandro

Published 2019

SKY WILLABEA
—PRESS—

ISBN: 978-1-7338402-3-1 (Paperback)

ISBN: 978-1-7338402-2-4 (Ebook)

Published by Sky Willabea Press

Nati Carrillo was inspired to write this book for JMV, her miracle who came before time.
"Never underestimate the power these little miracles bring to family dynamics."

This book is dedicated to every parent who was once afraid to hold their premature baby. For the unconditional love you gave and the suffering you endured and, for that moment, when you held your baby in your arms and realized that love conquers all!

When God made you, he didn't know yet, what to do.

He knew you'd be special, that much he knew.

He was way too excited that he rushed to make you.

He left out regret that much you and I can bet,
but once he got started, he couldn't stop yet.

He wanted you here today, not tomorrow
so he may have used glue instead of human tissue.

When you finally arrived; all tiny and fragile,
and yes, even a bit blue; it was no mistake.
Jesus knew you'd pull through.

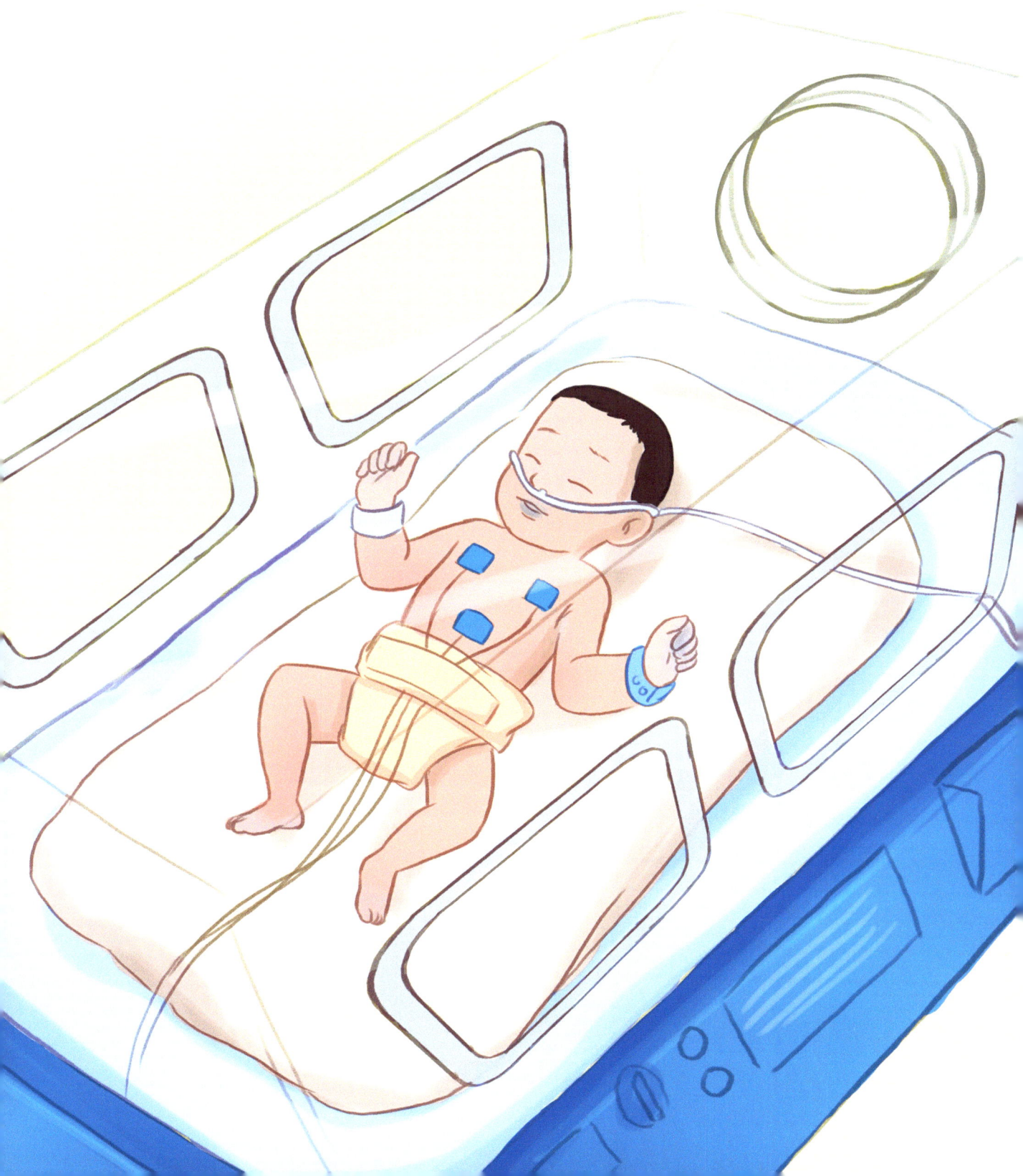

He gave you unlimited strength,
and then added to you the heart of a Saint
to spread love like fire, and get rid of all hate.

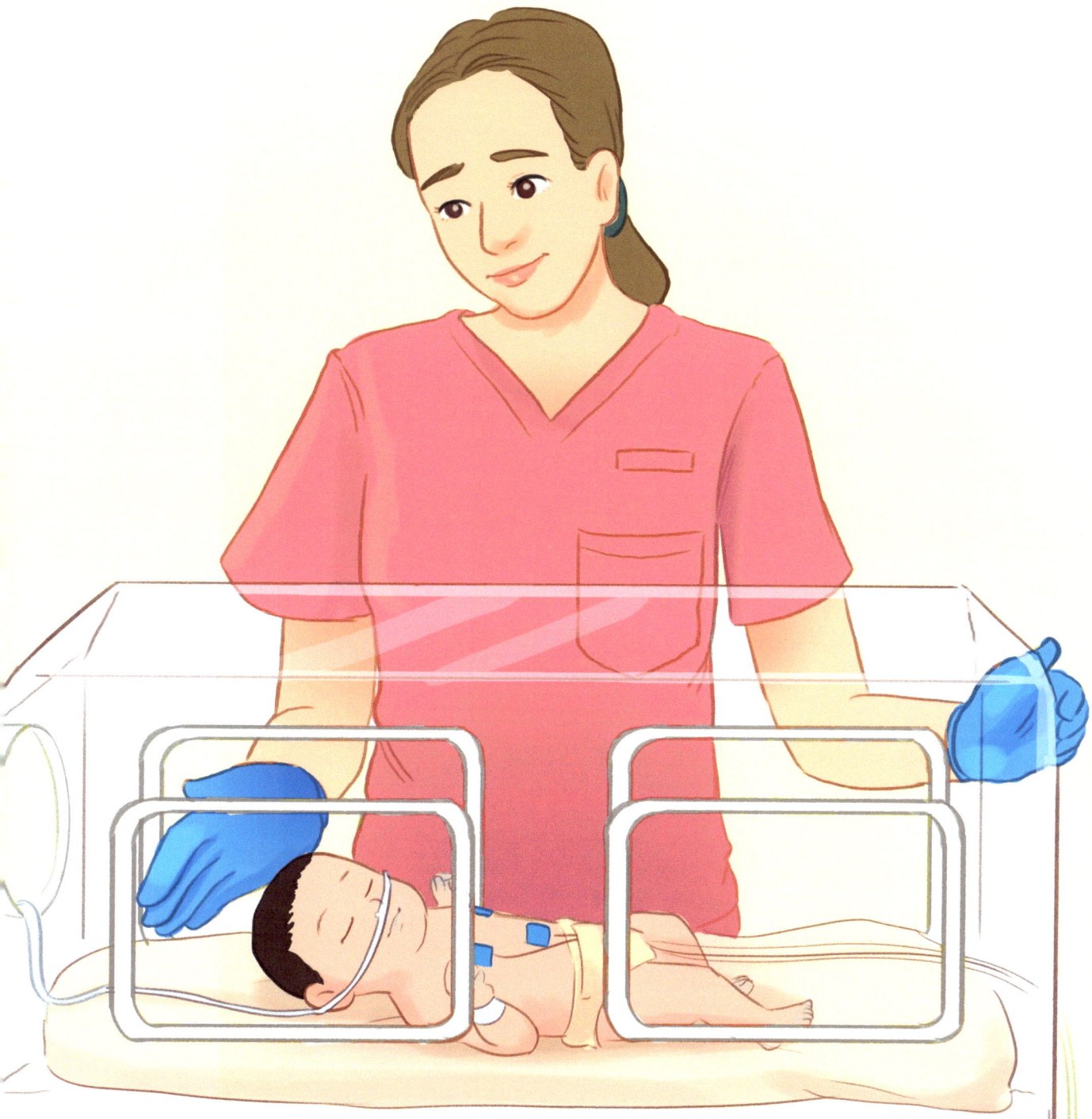

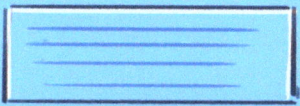

5 lbs

Oh, but he didn't stop there.
He continues to prove,
just look at you now,
still, a bit small but standing quite tall.

He tried to wait patiently for you
to start sharing his love
and prove to the world
that dreams do come true from above.
When you made your grand entrance,
he finally saw this beautiful creation of life.

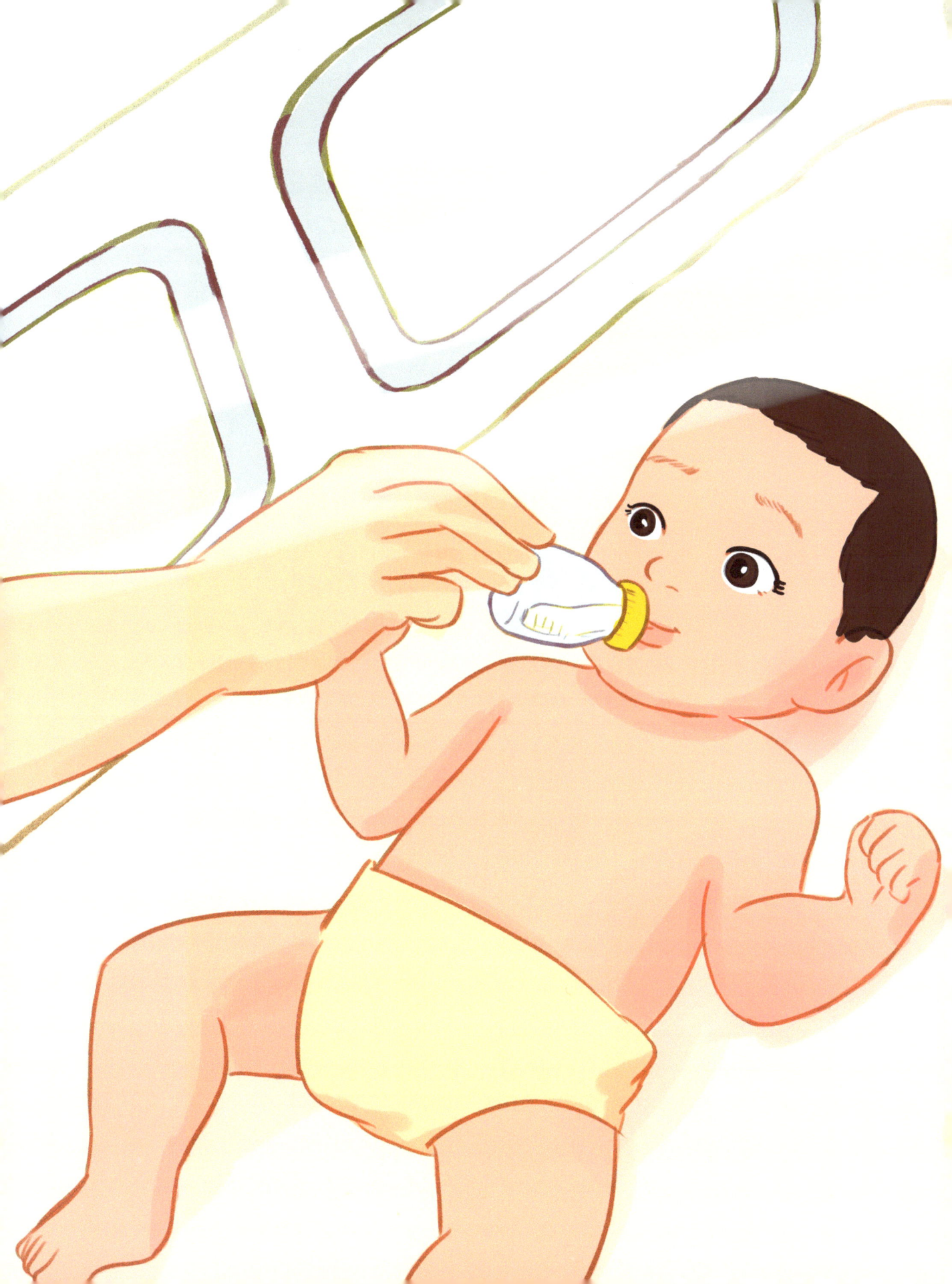

He smiled so proudly at this tiny new miracle.
Few are the chosen, he whispered,
and he undoubtedly knew.
That before you took your first breath
you'd be one of the selected few.

**And you have NO idea what we had to go through,
but know, that you were all worth it.
And we really truly love you!**

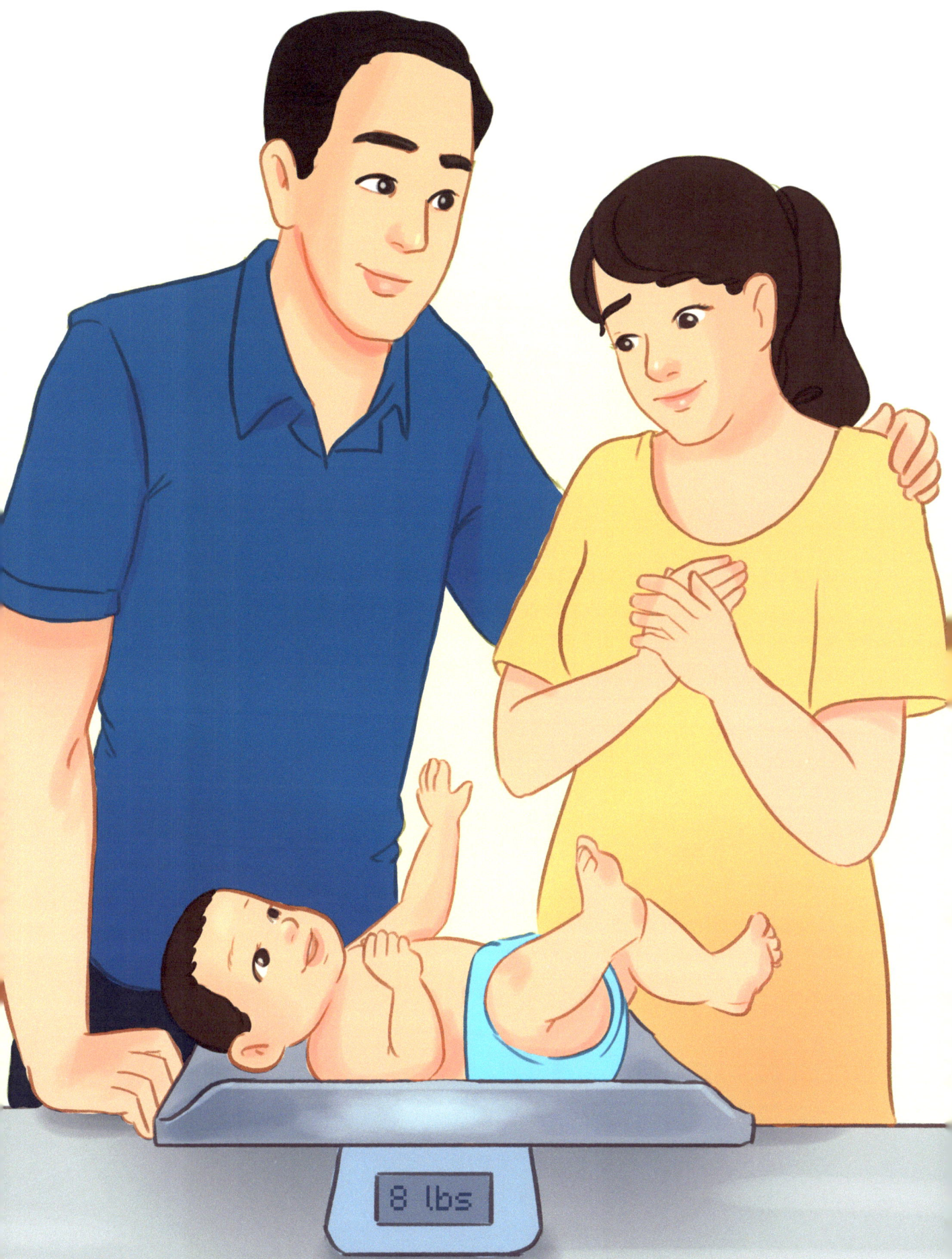
8 lbs

But none of that mattered because we were just
so excited to finally have and hold you!

About the author:

Nati Carrillo was born in Edcouch, Texas. Married with four children. She is a graduate of the University of Texas at Brownsville with a Master's degree in nursing with a specialty in nursing education. She is a Board-Certified Family Nurse Practitioner. She has written three fiction books: Bullies Create Bullies, a fiction/biography, The Slippery Slopes of Consequences, a fiction story of irony, and Shattered, a dark fiction story about how a young girl's abused life haunts her into her teenage years.

www.ingramcontent.com/pod-product-compliance
Lightning Source LLC
Chambersburg PA
CBHW042107040426

42448CB00002B/176